Hannah Elizabeth James is a HCPC certified music therapist from Kent, working with children in schools as well as with adults and children in Hospice care. She found her passion for singing and performing in 2002 when she was eight years old and has since performed solos at the Royal Albert Hall and the London Palladium. In 2019, she began her music therapy master's while working at hospice in the weald supporting patients with legacy work, writing songs, poems, and short stories. She hopes to continue supporting patients, children, and their loved ones through creative interventions and her newfound passion for writing.

HANNAH ELIZABETH

THE DAY THE EARTH GREW STRONGER

AUSTIN MACAULEY PUBLISHERS™
LONDON • CAMBRIDGE • NEW YORK • SHARJAH

Copyright © Hannah Elizabeth 2024

The right of **Hannah Elizabeth** to be identified as author of this work has been asserted by the author in accordance with sections 77 and 78 of the Copyright, Designs and Patents Act 1988.

All rights reserved. No part of this publication may be reproduced, stored in a retrieval system, or transmitted in any form or by any means, electronic, mechanical, photocopying, recording, or otherwise, without the prior permission of the publishers.

Any person who commits any unauthorised act in relation to this publication may be liable to criminal prosecution and civil claims for damages.

A CIP catalogue record for this title is available from the British Library.

ISBN 9781035834051 (Paperback)
ISBN 9781035834068 (Hardback)
ISBN 9781035834075 (ePub e-book)

www.austinmacauley.com

First Published 2024
Austin Macauley Publishers Ltd®
1 Canada Square
Canary Wharf
London
E14 5AA

I would like to dedicate this book to my husband, Billy James, my mother, Sandra Johnstone and my dear friend, Christie Monahan, for their continuous support and inspiring my work.

I would like to acknowledge Austin Macauley Publishers.

When someone you know and love, dies
It might feel hard to say your goodbyes

Their body is empty, their breathing has stopped
They're not coming back, but it's not your fault

You might be angry, or scared, or sad
You might be confused and feeling bad

It's okay to ask for support and to say how you feel
To help things make sense while you're trying to heal

You might be wondering,
"Where have they gone?"
And though they're not coming back,
They're memory lives on

Remember the earth connects you and your loved one
It's them who are keeping the earth so strong

Think of your loved one as part of the earth
And everywhere you go, you see their worth
They help the flowers to grow and thrive
They help the sun and moon to shine

They are the oxygen, rocks and trees
They are nature, the ocean and the breeze

They are the soil, they are the sky
They are the reason the Earth can survive

Though you can't see them,
they are always with you
In your heart, in your thoughts
and part of the earth too.

THE END